Foreword

Having known The Evansville Christian Life Center and Gina closely for many years, I was not surprised by the ability of this book to capture the depth of understanding, knowledge and love they have for the Evansville community.

The Community I See is a wonderfully written journey into the scope, misperceptions and real issues that our communities, and especially Evansville, face. Having spent my career seeking to realize the potential of organizations serving to make society better, I personally connect with Gina's vision of hope that allows people and communities to flourish into their greatest design. A community and an individual's potential does not get realized due to an intervention program, it happens when we choose, as Gina says, to be a neighbor.

When we choose to care, choose to love, choose to be in relationship, we choose greatness. The Evansville Christian Life Center chooses greatness and this book provides an excellent map for those who also are choosing to transform their community by being a great neighbor.

- Jamie Levy, President and Director of Vision, JDLevy & Associates

{ WHY I HAVE *hope* FOR A *better* EVANSVILLE }

GINA GIBSON

Executive Director of the Evansville Christian Life Center

with JEREMY SECREST

Special thanks to Damon Hancock, Jamie Levy, Robert Lupton, Rachel Mathew, Madison Nicholson, Stephen Ralph, Josey Roth, Sharon Taylor, and Marie Whitenack for their contributions to this project and to the many clients, staff, board, volunteers, and advocates who work to bring hope to our community.

ISBN-13: 978-0692920367 (Evansville Christian Life Center)

EVANSVILLE CHRISTIAN
LIFE CENTER
Evansville Christian Life Center
509 South Kentucky Avenue
Evansville, Indiana 47714-1091
restoringpeople.com
812.423.9222
@restoringpeople

Contents

What do you see? 1

West side of the West Side 2

Potential 6

Monica 9

Barriers, adversity, and hope 12

The answer 14

Being a neighbor 15

Being a neighbor...values what's best for my neighbor 16

Being a neighbor...listens first, helps second 22

Being a neighbor...addresses root causes, not just symptoms 24

Being a neighbor...looks at long-term success 28

Being a neighbor...collaborates 30

Being a neighbor...frees people toward their unique potential 34

Being a neighbor...points to Jesus 40

Being a neighbor...leads to flourishing 44

Action leads to hope 46

Hope 47

What do you see?

When you look at our community, what do you see?

Many see fear, hopelessness, and poverty. They see us labeled as fat and miserable. They see problems of drugs, health, and housing.

Not me.

Yes, those things are real. They're not what I see, though.

I see a community of hope.

Today's problems don't have to have the final word. Today could instead redeem tomorrow. Our kids could inherit a more safe, more healthy, and more vibrant community.

The choice is ours.

I invite you to step into a dream of what could be and a path toward making that a reality.

West side of the West Side

First off, I grew up in Mount Vernon. It's the west side of the West Side. So I appreciate the East-Siders letting me cross the border without a visa. I've even acclimated to the culture with kale shakes and carrots instead of Ski and Grippo's. Since we've been married, my husband and I have moved from Mt. Vernon, to the East Side, to Newburgh, and now to the North Side. We consider ourselves multi-cultural Evansvillians.

Whether you're West Side, East Side, Downtown, or any of the surrounding area, we are all part of a community. We share Don Mattingly, US 41, the Ohio River, walking trails, restaurants, concerts, stoplights on an expressway, and the Fall Festival. We share businesses, local government, and weather reports. We share friends, families, churches, groups, neighbors, and funerals.

We share each other's lives. As with family, like 'em or not, we're stuck with each other.

Because we share each other's lives like family, we also share problems:
- *Divorce*
- *Drugs*
- *Health*
- *Poverty*
- *Housing*
- *Education*
- *Brain sandwiches (Just kidding. Kind of.)*

Some stats back up the seriousness of a few of these problems:

1. *Over 40% of households within the city limits make less than $30,000 per year*
   [Data USA. www.datausa.io]
2. *On average, there are 495 homeless individuals on any given night*
   [2016 Point-in-Time Count Region 12]
3. *A worker must work 82 hours a week at minimum wage to afford a two bedroom apartment*
   [Out of Reach 2016 Pg. 73 http://nlihc.org/sites/default/files/oor/OOR_2016.pdf]
4. *60% of EVSC students are eligible for reduced or free meal programs*
   [www.in.gov - http://www.in.gov/sboe/files/EVSC_For_SBOE_12-3-14.pdf]
5. *1 out of every 5 people in Evansville is living in poverty*
   [United States Census Bureau, 2011-2015]
6. *Poverty has increased by 66% since the year 2000 in Vanderburgh County*
   [Division of United States Census Bureau, 2015]
7. *34% of Tri-State residents are considered obese*
8. *11% of Tri-State adults have misused prescription painkillers*
9. *19% of the region did not have healthcare coverage at some point in the course of a year*
10. *Over ⅓ of adults in the Tri-State region have high blood pressure*
11. *A high rate of depression affects adults in the Tri-State region*
12. *Many adults face obstacles to buying fresh produce, such as cost and transportation*
13. *Almost 25% of area children were diagnosed with developmental, emotional, and/or behavioral problems*

*[Welborn Baptist Foundation, Inc. (2015). Tri-State Health Survey, 2015 TSHS]

Like family, when we share each other's lives long enough, we start getting used to the problems. We can yell until we're blue in the face, but sometimes those nasty habits don't go away. There doesn't seem to be change. Or at least the change doesn't seem worth it.

We've tried that. It didn't work. So we decide to live with it.

For instance, Uncle Darren's alcohol problem didn't go away after the intervention. He gave it a good try for three months, but it came back. Rosie's temper still gets her in trouble even though you took them to a counselor. Grandma Betty's five food groups are potato chips, chocolate, cheeseburgers, fries, and soda, even after the heart attack.

Sometimes change doesn't happen.

What if it's because we tried solving the problem in a wrong way? Maybe Uncle Darren's alcohol problem isn't beyond fixing. Maybe an intervention just wasn't the way to resolve it.

What if the problems we're facing in our community don't have the final word? Could it be, that even though we've been working really hard, we haven't been working on the right things? What if the problems of despair, health, and poverty can be solved? Maybe we just need a new perspective on how to fix them.

As I've led the Evansville Christian Life Center for over a decade, I feel like I've had a front row seat to our city. The good, the bad, and everything in between. I've had the privilege of meeting with homeless families, interacting with city officials, collaborating with nonprofit staff, talking with law enforcement, and partnering with business leaders. Through all of this come countless stories of despair as well as a surprising number of stories of *hope*.

Through it all, hope continues to emerge. To be honest, hope shines brighter than despair.

Not a hope of groundless dreaming, but one that's rooted in truth and reality.

This **hope** is what I want to share with you.

Hope shines
brighter than
despair.

Potential

The community I see can be summed up in one word: **potential**.

Before we get to that, however, let's look at another word: **flourishing**.
(Hey, they're both great words.)

While we can argue about what it looks like and how to get there, I'd guess pretty much all of us can agree we'd like to live in a flourishing community. One where all areas of culture are healthy and operating for the common good. One where all people, regardless of color, age, gender, economic status, or social standing have the opportunity to pursue their potential.

Think about what our community could look like if we're each free to move toward our potential.

I see:
- *Exceptional teachers helping raise up the next generation to live better lives than their parents*
- *Business leaders creating thriving places of work and innovation*
- *Artists deepening our lives with powerful art*
- *Parents equipped to raise their children in a loving and healthy environment*
- *Marriages strong enough to bring a stable home life to our kids*
- *Generosity as a way of life*
- *Churches working together to better the community*
- *Every single person donating large gifts to fund the Evansville Christian Life Center (Just throwing that one out there!)*

It's easy to think that because we live in America, everyone has the opportunity to do pursue their potential. On paper, we technically do. Yet, the reality is that many have barriers keeping them from the opportunity to move toward their potential. Some of these barriers are nearly insurmountable for someone to overcome by themselves. Circumstances, lack of education, and lack of awareness can cripple someone's pursuit of their potential.

When anyone doesn't live up to their potential, we all suffer. We miss out on the goodness their unique life was created to offer the world. That goodness can be anything from a beautiful smile, to an innovative product, to maintaining law and order, to humor, to keeping accurate books.

For those of us in the suburbs, it might be hard to grasp, but these barriers exist in our own community.

Some of these barriers include:
- *Generational poverty*
- *Relational poverty*
- *Situational poverty*
- *Lack of access to healthy food*
- *Lack of transportation*
- *Lack of safe, affordable housing*
- *Addiction issues*

For those of us without much exposure to the problems of poverty, overcoming these things may seem like a matter of simple logistics.

- *"If you can't get to work, get a closer job."*
- *"Find a cheaper apartment"*
- *"Take the bus to the grocery store."*

I'd like to challenge your thinking; many people in these circumstances are living in a different world than you and me. We may be just a mile away from each other, but the everyday realities of our lives could not be more different.

Yet, there is still hope for everyone to pursue their potential.

Monica

Monica is a single mother of three. She lived for several years on government assistance, but decided she wanted more for her family. Circumstances seemed to dictate her life up to that point, but they would not dictate her future. Coming from a family in poverty herself, developing a mindset to move forward was difficult enough. It was a completely new outlook and paradigm. Actually doing the work of moving out of poverty was going to be even harder.

However, Monica had grit.

"I've had enough," she said. "My family's poverty ends with me."

Monica got a job earning minimum wage at a restaurant on the far east side. She was excited at this first step.

Even though she lived in Jacobsville, her determination drove her to make it work. Each morning would find her up at 4:30 getting breakfast ready for her kids. Then, it was out the door by 5:30, walk the kids to her sister's house, and catch the city bus at 5:55. An hour later she'd step off her final bus where the route ended. She would finish her commute with a half-mile walk to the restaurant. Despite rain, ice, and snow, she made it work. Her dream of living with her kids in a home she owned drove her forward. Monica wasn't taking "no" for an answer.

She worked hard, did a great job, and was offered a promotion a few months later. Her persistence paid off with a new position and a pay raise.

She figured things out with her sister to watch the kids earlier so she could be at the restaurant by 5 a.m. She found she had a knack for leadership and excelled in her new position. Things were looking up.

However, a few weeks later she received notice from her Section 8 housing. Because her pay increased, she lost her subsidized housing allowance, and her rent increased $400 per month. The increase in pay she received wasn't enough to cover the increase in rent. The promotion actually made Monica financially worse off than before.

She was forced to step back to her previous role and despaired on how difficult this climb was actually going to be.

- *"I could get a new job, but I don't yet have the skills for one that pays enough to get off assistance and provide for my kids."*
- *"I could get a second job, but my kids would be home alone in the evenings because my sister works second shift and I don't have any other options right now."*
- *"I could go to school online, but can't afford tuition and taking out a loan puts me even further behind."*
- *"What do I do?"*

The pull to slide back into her previous life was ever-present, requiring nothing from her but to settle.

"It's not where I want to be, but maybe that's my lot in life. It's too hard. Too confusing. Too stressful."

The barriers poverty brings are complex.

The barriers
poverty brings
are complex.

Barriers, adversity, and hope

Fixing these barriers that Monica and others run into requires much more than simple answers:

- "Get a job."
- "Pull yourself up by your bootstraps."
- "Go to school."

Often, our help from the outside does little to actually help her move forward:

- "Here is a free meal."
- "Here are free backpacks with school supplies."
- "Here are free clothes."

These things are nice. They're friendly. But they're not really accomplishing much to help Monica truly move forward. Unfortunately, they can also continue and reinforce the cycle of dependency she's working to overcome.

Monica's story is one of thousands. Individuals and families with their own histories, challenges, weaknesses, and circumstances are caught in the grip of poverty and need. The door to their potential, for a myriad of reasons, is locked. The key seems to be lost forever.

Adversity is not the problem. Adversity is part of life. It's a healthy part, teaching us and growing us in ways we wouldn't have discovered without it. The stories of our lives would be much less interesting without the conflict we're forced to deal with.

But if the doorway to potential seems forever locked, hope is lost.

Hope is too precious to lose.

When people in our community lose hope, for whatever reason, symptoms begin to emerge. Symptoms create circumstances. Circumstances become desperate. Desperate circumstances cause desperate actions. Those actions, from addiction to crime to abuse, break relationships. Broken relationships cause broken people who perpetuate and further this tragic cycle.

Poverty and its side effects are the source of many of the ills in our community.

The problem is not a lack of food, lack of clothing, or lack of money. These are circumstances.

The problem is a lack of hope.

That's true poverty.

The answer

At the Evansville Christian Life Center, we dream of a community with less poverty and stronger families. We exist for people like Monica. We have programs and services for those in her circumstances. We connect the Monica's of our community to other wonderful organizations who do things we don't.

But we're not the answer. Neither are the organizations we partner with.

You are.
So am I.

If we truly want a flourishing community, a place where Monica and her family can move toward their potential, then the answer is...

Being a neighbor.

Being a neighbor

Wait, stop! I saw you roll your eyes. Don't put the book down. There's more to being a neighbor than meets the eye.

We all know we should be neighbors, just like we all know we should live a healthy lifestyle.

Knowing we should live a healthy lifestyle, however, doesn't mean that:
- *We actually live a healthy lifestyle*
- *We really know what a healthy lifestyle looks like*

Let's take a journey to explore some new perspectives on what it means to be a neighbor. A fresh perspective could make a marked difference in whether we catch a vision for hope or instead slide back into doing the same things expecting different results.

Being a neighbor...
values what's best for my neighbor

Have you noticed a weird thing that happens when we talk about helping someone out?

We talk about **our** efforts:
- "We collected 18,000,000 canned goods."
- "We donated $5,000 to a local charity."
- "We handed out 2,738 backpacks to kids going to school."

Don't get me wrong, these are great things. And it's good to celebrate the efforts of a church or organization when they pull together to do something generous.

But what are these stats about?

Ourselves.

It's really easy for our giving to be about us. Whether training our kids, showing our corporate impact, or reaching out as a church, we want to be generous. Generous is good.

However, only measuring our own efforts doesn't necessarily lead to results.

Let's say I'm a sales rep and my manager gives me a goal to land 100 accounts. I decide sending out postcards to potential clients is a good way to land those accounts, so I send out 10,000 postcards. That's a lot of postcards. I decide that's not enough, so I spend the rest of my budget to send out 10,000 more. I decide I need to go all out, and ask my manager for an increased budget. I then send out 10,000 more.

"Check it out! I sent out 30,000 postcards!"

"Who cares how many postcards you sent out, Gina? How many accounts have you landed?"

If my end goal is not results, then it's possible for my work to be a waste.

Real generosity isn't about us or how much we give. Real generosity is in how it affects the person who receives it. Real generosity is not about finding a person to receive OUR gift, but about discovering what that person needs and helping them find that.

Beyond that, an even tougher truth to swallow is that some of the ways we give actually hurt those we give to.

Not to burst your bubble, but:
- *Free food and clothing often lead to dependency and enabling of those we serve*
- *Backpacks full of food and school supplies put some children in a potentially vulnerable position in certain families dealing with addictions, criminal activity, etc.*
- *Free Christmas toys for a family shame the father, making him feel unable to provide for his kids*

I don't mean to sound like a cynic, but this is simply the reality of how nice actions aren't necessarily kind. Guess what? At the Evansville Christian Life Center, we participated in each one of these services in the past. It wasn't out of selfish intent, condescending attitudes, or lack of effort. We simply didn't know.

Now, we're learning from our mistakes and working to move forward.

Being a neighbor is about helping someone move forward. Yes, it's meeting needs when appropriate (like an emergency), but ultimately it's about helping a person remove barriers that keep them from their potential.

So how do we help someone move toward their potential?

Fishing.

"You give a poor man a fish and you feed him for a day. You teach him to fish and you give him an occupation that will feed him for a lifetime."
- Chinese proverb

I actually hate to fish (it's difficult to do in high heels) and would rather play golf, but the principle of that Chinese proverb remains. At the ECLC, we usually say it like this: "a hand up, not a handout."

People struggling in poverty want the same thing we do, a flourishing community. They also have skills, insights, and relationships to bring to the team.

Think about it. If you were in these circumstances, how would you want to be helped? To have a "rich" person come in to do everything for you? To create a relationship where you were continually dependent on that person for your needs? Of course not.

You'd want a partner. Someone to work beside you as you move yourself forward. A coach, not a hero.

One of our services at the ECLC is called the GAIN Initiative. This is a community of both participants and partners working together to overcome poverty, both individually and as a community.

One of the things I love about visiting the GAIN Initiative is that it's often hard to determine who is a participant and who is a partner. They're aimed at the same goal, fighting poverty. They also both provide value as they work together to fight poverty. Participants need partners to help them pull themselves out of whatever situation they're in.

Let's be honest, we're all in need. I've yet to meet an upper or middle-class person who didn't have emotional, relational, spiritual, or even financial problems. We need to get over ourselves and admit we're all human, we're all in need, and we also all have value to offer this world.

Understanding this moves us out of "superhero syndrome," where we swoop down to rescue someone, and into simply being neighbors who help each other out. Give and take.

Once we can do that, we can begin to value what's best for our neighbor and work with them to discover and find that themselves.

(If you want to learn more about this concept, check out our friend Robert Lupton's popular book *Toxic Charity*. It's an easy, insightful, and challenging read.)

We're all human.
We're all in need.
We all have value
to offer this world.

Being a neighbor...
listens first, helps second

If we're going to value what's best for our neighbors, we have to admit we might not know best.

Have you been at a job where an executive comes in, looks at a department they aren't familiar with, and makes changes? All the people working in that department understand there's no way that change will work. They're close enough to the work to understand what's really behind the problems as well as fifty-seven other factors the executive doesn't know about.

It's easy for those trying to help their neighbors to act like that executive.

On the flip side, some organizations, like our friends at Community One, do what's called "community development." Community development focuses on improving a specific neighborhood, looking at it holistically, attempting to learn what the real problems are, and then working together with neighborhood leaders to determine solutions.

Do you know the first step of community development?

They host discussion events where they...
listen.

Community development organizations, even those who are experts in their field, don't come into a neighborhood assuming they know the best route to improvement. They gather neighborhood leaders and listen to them.

Guess what they find? Good ideas. Solutions to problems.
Concepts and plans they would not have found on their own.

Then, after a lot of listening, they begin organizing strategies, volunteers, contractors, building materials, and then comes the "work."

Results require the hard work of listening before you help.

Community development is about relationships and results.

So is being a neighbor.

Being a neighbor...
addresses root causes, not just symptoms

Let's go back to Monica. Monica's circumstances were complex. So was finding a solution to help her move forward.

Let's say you, like Monica, are a single parent. It's Monday, you're down to your last two diapers, and you don't get paid until Friday. You visit us at the ECLC. We do our best to help you or connect you to another organization if we can't. What if you came back two weeks later with the same problem? Then again two weeks later? Diapers are not your real problem. There is a deeper issue going on.

To help you, we'd get to know you and learn how you got into your circumstances. We'd begin to uncover barriers and recommend plans of action to move forward. Your need might actually be learning how to budget, finding a different job, figuring out affordable transportation, a mentor, new relationships, or maybe even joining our GAIN Initiative.

Having all the diapers in the world wouldn't help your deeper need.

This is why, at the ECLC, we focus our efforts on issues of poverty and families.

Like we said earlier, poverty is often a root cause for many symptoms in our society like abuse, addiction, and crime. Poverty also leads to broken families. In the same way, broken family situations, like an absentee dad or abusive mom, can cause circumstances which lead to poverty.

Poverty and broken families often go hand in hand.

These underlying causes often can't be found without relationship. It's messy. It's sticky. It can require complex solutions. But it works.

We see people move out of poverty for good. We see them thrive in their careers, take leadership roles in the community, and even work to help others on their journey out of poverty.

These are outcomes that can't be reached simply by giving away diapers.

So what role do diapers play?

Diapers are important! We just need to put them in their place. (No pun intended. Kind of.) A mom who needs diapers or food for their child today doesn't care about developing a budget. So what do diapers do? Diapers open the door to relationships (put that on a bumper sticker).

Relationships open the door to resources.

For us, that's shown in some of our services like the hot meal program and clothing department. Those with whom we are able to build a relationship are then invited to other resources like classes, coaching, and training. These resources equip them to move forward on their journey. Then, they're invited to take part in the more intensive GAIN Initiative.

It sounds so clean and tidy when I say it like that. It's really pretty messy, but it's working and people are moving out of poverty.

As we work to fight issues in our community as individuals, companies, churches, and organizations, the more we can address root causes, the more we will see lasting results.

We'll be better neighbors when we care enough to truly help.

Diapers open the door to relationships.

Being a neighbor...
looks at long-term success

Let's go back to Monica. Lasting success for Monica is not measured in a 3-month, 6-month, or even year-long span. In the short-term, we can begin to see wins like starting a savings account, paying off debts, establishing a budget, gaining parenting skills, developing a network of professional relationships.

Lasting success, however, looks at the bigger picture of Monica's life. It's seen in a 25-year span of her kids graduating high school, going to college or learning a trade, and then having a career. It's her children developing healthy relationships, having families of their own, making a difference to those around them, and raising their kids to do the same.

Monica could leave a legacy of flourishing that multiplies over time.

Let's look an even a broader picture. Monica is one person who affects one family who then affects the families around them. There are thousands of Monica's in our community. This ripple effect of flourishing continues with each person who is able to move forward toward their potential.

Quick fixes feel better because we see immediate results. However, they often unintentionally sabotage long-term success.

Working to develop neighborhoods, reverse cycles of generational poverty, or change perspectives cannot be done in a weekend service project blitz. A weekend blitz is a great step, but it's one step out of a thousand needed for lasting change.

Just like the story of "The Tortoise and the Hare," when it comes to fighting poverty and strengthening families, the tortoise wins in the long run.

If our community were full of individuals free to pursue their potential today, what would Evansville look like in twenty-five years?

Being a neighbor...
collaborates

"When we work together we all get better." - Jeremiah Jettison

Once we value the best in our neighbors and listen, there comes a time to take action.

However, when that time comes, here's what often happens:
- *"We want to reach those in need. Let's start a food pantry." - Group A*
- *"We want to help serve the community, let's begin a food pantry." - Group B*
- *"You know what would help our city? A food pantry. Let's start one!" - Group C*

Did you know Evansville has over eighty food pantries?

Eighty! I'm not kidding.

While that's a sign of generosity, the bigger question is do we need that many food pantries?

- *Would it have made more sense for some of them to have partnered with an existing food pantry instead of starting their own?*
- *Would it make sense for some of them to merge?*
- *Would it make sense for some of them to close and do something else?*

I mean no disrespect and have no room to judge. We had a food pantry for 30 years until we replaced it recently with a Food Co-op.

The question isn't about food pantries. The question is when we are compelled to work on an issue like hunger, why do we feel the need to start something ourselves? Why don't we instead first partner with someone who already does that work?

Did you know the Evansville area has literally hundreds of nonprofits working on social issues? At the ECLC, we partner with over 160. From job skills training, to sex trafficking, to at-risk youth programs, there is a tremendous amount of fantastic work being done.

These organizations have experience, relationships, and knowledge in dealing with the issues they address. They also need the support of volunteers and donors to further their work.

For some reason, almost no one seems to be aware that they exist.

I've heard too many times in church leadership meetings, *"There's nothing being done about homelessness in Evansville."*

- *Did you know that our friends at Aurora have an entire organization dedicated solely to fighting homelessness in our community?*
- *Did you know there's a City/County Commission on Homelessness?*
- *Did you know hundreds of people and organizations come together each spring for an event called Vanderburgh Homeless Connect?*

I'm afraid many of us are simply unaware of the abundance of opportunities to join work that's already being done. We need to do our homework before jumping in.

How do you learn about these places? Contact United Way. Contact us at the ECLC. Ask nonprofit staff members in town. They most likely know how to connect you.

That being said, I do understand why churches and other organizations start their own thing. It's much simpler. You can do it according to your own values. You can get it up and running quickly. You can set the rules. You can work with your friends.

But what is the goal? If it's measuring our efforts like we talked about earlier ("We gave away 18,000,000 canned goods."), then it works better.

If, however, our goal is valuing what's best for our neighbors and making a difference in the issue we're tackling, then maybe we should pause before starting something ourselves. We can often make a bigger difference by partnering with others.

What if, as we meet on an outreach or missions committee, our goal isn't about what we give, but the results it will create? What if, before taking action, we begin by listening to those who are already working in that area and see if there are opportunities to collaborate? Even if we start your own thing, we might develop a relationship and find opportunities to partner as we work together on the issue.

Don't get me wrong.

There are plenty of good reasons to start something new. Many area nonprofits, ours included, were started by churches and organizations. Let's just make sure we're not unnecessarily reinventing the wheel. Instead, let's concentrate on furthering the actual causes we're working for.

I understand everyone else's agenda isn't ours. But what if we set aside a part of our agenda to help others with theirs?

What if...
- *the issue we're trying to fight is more important than our metrics?*
- *it's more important than our PR?*
- *it's more important than if everyone on the team agrees with our theological distinctives?*

In our overly sensitive society, we seem to search out reasons to be offended by someone else and withdraw from them. Maybe that's part of the problem.

What if...
- *there is an incredible opportunity for us to sacrifice a little of our own preferences, organizational distinctives, or programs to create a better whole community?*
- *we join someone else's project instead of inviting them to ours?*
- *we help them work on it instead of just affirming it?*
- *we discover collaboration is part of being a neighbor?*

It may bring up arguments. It may bring up differences of opinion. It may bring up frustration. Just like any relationship.

It's simply the give and take of neighbors.

What if the process of going through that hard work yields more understanding, more empathy, more respect, deeper relationships, and ultimately, a better community?

I think that's worth it.

Being a neighbor...
frees people toward their unique potential

Walk down Franklin Street any evening at the Fall Festival and look at the incredible diversity of people:
- *Introverts and extroverts*
- *Dark skin, light skin, and in-between skin*
- *Those with beards and those with shaved heads*
- *Urban, suburban, and rural*
- *Fast and slow walkers*
- *Fast and slow talkers*
- *Liberals and conservatives*
- *Young and old*
- *Those eating brain sandwiches and those sick from eating brain sandwiches*
- *People who give really big gifts to the Evansville Christian Life Center and those who are getting ready to...*

Each of us has unique value to offer the world around us.

Think back to the people who have made a difference in your life.
How did they provide value to you?
- *Ideas*
- *Smiles*
- *Respect*
- *Service*
- *Mentoring*
- *Friendship*
- *Hospitality*
- *Love*
- *Kindness*
- *Accounting*
- *Mechanics*
- *Engineering*
- *Art*
- *Music*
- *Plumbing*
- *Computer programming*
- *Leadership*
- *Understanding*

Chances are some of them made a difference in very practical and tangible ways. They taught you a new perspective. They trained you with a new skill. They gave you an opportunity. Some of them probably made a difference more relationally. They listened to you. They told you the truth even when it hurt. They were simply there for you. Some of them might have helped in ways that are harder to describe, but made a profound difference. Their smile made you feel respected. Their compliment changed the course of a tough day. Their example inspired you to reach further.

To grasp this concept gives new meaning to the value we can each provide. It's easy to slip into the pattern of our culture and define worth or value by simplistic things like financial success, ability to produce, or sexual attractiveness.

There is a higher way.

To move far beyond Evansville, many in our community have taken trips to East Asia through our friends at Uncharted. They go there to serve orphans in one of the poorest areas of the world.

You know what's odd about that? Those who go to serve orphans come back saying they received more than they gave. These children who only have a couple outfits to their name have value and worth to offer the very people who go to serve them.

That sounds like neighbors who happen to live halfway across the world.

Think about value in a broader context.

We talked earlier about the importance of everyone pursuing their potential. Understanding the value each person has to offer helps us understand what that potential looks like. Someone living out their potential can be an incredibly unique thing. It probably doesn't look like you or me.

When we have a more holistic understanding of the value of each person, then we begin to understand why it's so vital that each person in our community has the opportunity to pursue his or her potential. We need everyone's contribution. Whether that contribution is giving a smile, discovering the cure for cancer, or being present, we need every person.

When someone is not free to pursue their potential, we all lose.

Now, let's take that one step further.

As a follower of Jesus, I look to the Bible as God's revealed word to us. In those Scriptures, we see over and over again the concept that all human beings are made by the Creator with equal and inestimable worth. We are each created in the image of God. His worth is living in our skin by the simple fact that we are human.

That's why, as an organization founded upon the teachings of Jesus, we believe in the value of every human being. From the marginalized student, to the drug addict, to the corporate executive, to the unborn child, to the single mother struggling to raise her children, to the working-class individual who may at different times of his life be a donor or a client, to the mentally challenged senior needing a meal to make the budget stretch further, each has worth, value, and potential.

We don't define their potential, we help them discover it.

Just like the Mesker Park Zoo and Botanic Garden is a beautiful display of diverse shapes, colors, sizes, and textures from animals and plants, our community can be a beautiful display of the diversity of people pursuing their potential.

Who wouldn't want to be part of that?

When someone
is not free to
pursue their
potential,
we all lose.

Being a neighbor...
points to Jesus

Whoa, wait! Don't get angry or weird when I mention Jesus, just hear me out.

I'm picturing three reactions to what I just said:
- *"Christians are ignorant, mean, and clueless. I'm putting this book down."*
- *"It's about time! I wondered if you were even Christians."*
- *"I'm curious, tell me more."*

Regardless of your thoughts on religion, church, or Christianity, the person Jesus caused a quite a stir. Many of the establishments in our world came as a result of people following his teachings, from the abolition of slavery to schools to hospitals.

Jesus called out hypocrisy, pride, lust, and revenge. He talked about serving the needy, about having a pure heart, and about living together in peace.

Jesus also went further and claimed that he was God in person. The embodiment of God as a human. The book of Matthew states that Jesus was the fulfillment of an ancient prophecy which said, "the people dwelling in darkness have seen a great light, and for those dwelling in the region and shadow of death, on them a light has dawned." (*ESV*, Matthew 4:16)

Jesus offered a new way of life from what they had previously known. Changing from selfishness to love, from external practices to purity of heart, from laws to relationship, he turned their existing way of thinking upside down and in some ways told them those things which they thought brought them life did not. He then said, "I am the way, the truth, and the life." (*KJV*, John 14:6)

Jesus said an interesting phrase, "the kingdom of heaven is at hand." (*ESV*, Matthew 4:17) He then taught people to pray, "your kingdom come, your will be done, on earth as it is in heaven." (*NIV*, Matthew 6:10)

The kingdom of heaven is this new way of life. A way that not only offers life after death, but life today. The idea that success, money, fame, beauty, sex, pleasure, power, peace, or happiness—the things we think will bring us life—do not. Instead, this new way of life is taking the way of heaven, where God and His characteristics of love, justice, mercy, and beauty are fully realized, and bringing it here to earth. Our pursuit of life and love are found in Him.

It's not just a way of life, it's a life of relationship with God. Without Jesus, our sin, the evil which causes us to pursue our needs outside of God, keeps us from that life. Jesus opened the door to that life through his death, burial, and resurrection from the dead. He conquered sin and death, made payment for our sin, and offers an open door to the kingdom of heaven. Death and evil do not have the final word.

Life and love do.

So, as followers of Jesus, we work to bring love, justice, mercy, and beauty to the world we live in. We're "citizens" of the kingdom of heaven and live out our new identities by bringing life and love wherever we go. We work to make things in Evansville, as it is in heaven.

"Yeah, right. Those aren't the Christians I know."

Here's the deal—we're still human. We make mistakes, we judge people, we sin, we get too political, we retreat. We act like, well, we act like humans. The disease of sin still clings to our minds and affects our hearts and actions.

Scripture points to the fact that for those who follow Jesus, death is not the end, but is a new beginning. There is life now and life eternal as we step fully into heaven and are fully present with God. A place where there is no evil, no death, and no suffering.

So we live it out now as best we can, trying to open doors that shine the light of heaven into our souls and into the world. The reality is that those doors can't open all the way while evil and death are a part of our world.

That's a really long, but important detour to explain why being a good neighbor points to Jesus.

For those of who you do not consider yourselves followers of Jesus, I doubt a couple pages of explanation will suddenly make you decide to change. I do hope, however, that it helps you understand where we're coming from. It hopefully gives you a glimpse of why we do what we do. With that, please know, regardless of your beliefs, we'd love to have you join us in our work.

We're not working to get a bonus at a great sales convention in the sky, not trying to move everyone to a certain political party, and not trying to get you to wear a religious bracelet.

We're trying to live out our new identities as representatives of this kingdom of heaven.

So back to being neighbors...

Jesus said to love our neighbor as ourselves.

That's a pretty tall order and goes back to some of the earlier things we talked about being a neighbor, valuing what's best for them, listening, freeing them to pursue their unique potential.

Jesus also said that everyone we come in contact with is our neighbor. Even our enemies. Even West Siders and East Siders.

So, at the Evansville Christian Life Center, our programs are centered around love, justice, mercy, and beauty. We want to bring those things to our neighbors. It's how and why we love.

Our programs, from the Food Co-op, to the Health Clinic, to the GAIN Initiative are designed to help people remove barriers that keep them from their potential. From clients, to volunteers, to staff, to board members, to donors, we hope that Jesus is seen, shown, and known. We consider ourselves a small community of peers all trying to help restore people from need to potential in Christ.

If what we believe is true, and we have so many evidences that it is, we simply can't be authentic neighbors without pointing to Jesus.

Being a neighbor...
leads to flourishing

Earlier, we talked about flourishing.

This idea of flourishing actually comes from a term used in the Bible:

"Shalom."

It's a word Jews use to greet each other.

It means wholeness, perfection, prosperity, and peace. Some people sum this up in the word "flourishing."

Through this word we see God's original design for creation, harmony, beauty, provision, relationship.

Yet, because of evil within and without, humans broke this flourishing and relationship with God. Evil and death destroyed this shalom and opened the door to pain, heartache, death, abuse, addiction, war, crime, and all things that stand in contrast to God's original design.

Our design is still for shalom. So we work toward flourishing in our homes, our neighborhoods, and our cities. However imperfectly, we work toward making our businesses, relationships, churches, governments, schools, nonprofits, families, and neighborhoods flourish.

This flourishing is far richer than a simplistic American dream vision of prosperity where we all live in big houses, drive nice cars, and don't have any problems. It's a more honest and human vision of prospering. It's a vision where the qualities of the kingdom of heaven come more clearly into view.

As long as evil and death are on the earth, shalom won't be fully seen. That, however, doesn't keep us from working toward establishing as much of it as possible here on earth.

It's who we are. It's what we do.

In Evansville, as it is in heaven.

Action leads to hope

When people begin to take action, flourishing begins to take root.

When...
- *a place like Haynie's Corner transitions from an unsafe drug hotspot into a vibrant arts district with fantastic restaurants, shops, and galleries*
- *a local plastics company intentionally sets a percentage of their revenues to make a difference here and around the world*
- *a business leader lets her team members volunteer at a charity on company time*
- *J.E. Shekell chooses to do our heating and A/C work at no cost for nearly 20 years*
- *Welborn Hospital created the Welborn Foundation, which now invests significant funds in local efforts addressing community needs*
- *an executive serves on a board of directors*
- *a 10-year-old asks for cash for Christmas and donates it to our Food Co-op*
- *a skilled craftsman donates his lunch hour to hang a sign*
- *a mom watches a neighbor's child*
- *a hard conversation happens respectfully*
- *a couple decides to hold on to their marriage*
- *someone reaches across party, religious, ideological, or racial lines to form a friendship*
- *a single mom decides poverty ends with her*

Flourishing requires action. Neighboring requires action. Love requires action.

Hope

We've taken quite a ride from poverty to neighbors to Shalom to brain sandwiches.

Thanks for taking the time to read with me. This book is about hope, specifically why I have hope for a better community.

I have hope that, when we overcome misunderstandings, grasp a bigger picture of Jesus and flourishing, and begin to take action on what we learn, that the root causes of problems in our community will begin to heal.

When the roots heal, things can begin to bloom.

But if the roots don't heal, decay will take over.

We're at a crossroads in our community where enough cultivation has taken place that we're on the verge of exciting movements forward. However, those movements won't gain traction, if we don't act.

If we stay where we are, I'm afraid Evansville could spiral downward. Lack of innovation. Lack of progress. Lack of neighbors. Isolation. Silos of people and organizations solely looking out for their own interests.

That would lead to increased crime, less effective education, young people leaving for better opportunities, fewer quality jobs, increased poverty, more divorce, greater health concerns, more broken families, increased racism, unfunded nonprofits, solvable issues growing into epidemics, failing churches, poor self-worth, lack of art, lack of innovation, and a decay that ultimately breaks our community further apart.

With action, however, we can reverse this trend.

This crossroads we're at could move Evansville into an exciting and vibrant future we've only dreamed of. Our kids and grandkids could grow up with a new community.

The choice is ours.

It starts with individuals...like Monica.

Monica represents several people we've met through our work. We've changed some details around, but her story is not over-dramatic or embellished.

The good news is the real people we based her off of have taken steps forward, with many of them actually stepping out of poverty for good. Several have taken part in our GAIN Initiative to walk through the complex situations they were in. Several are now community leaders making a difference in others' lives. Their children have both a different present and a different future because the trajectory of their parents' lives completely changed.

Story after story, life after life, all pointing to hope.

I believe this could be the story of our community.

We've been in captivity so long, we may not know what freedom looks like. We may not dare to hope. But hope is based on truth. True hope is attainable.

The prophet Jeremiah said the following words of God to the people of Israel when they were captives in Babylon, and they apply equally to us:

This is what the Lord Almighty, the God of Israel, says to all those I carried into exile from Jerusalem to Babylon: "Build houses and settle down; plant gardens and eat what they produce. Marry and have sons and daughters; find wives for your sons and give your daughters in marriage, so that they too may have sons and daughters. Increase in number there; do not decrease. Also, seek the peace and prosperity of the city to which I have carried you into exile. Pray to the Lord for it, because if it prospers, you too will prosper."

...This is what the Lord says: "When seventy years are completed for Babylon, I will come to you and fulfill my good promise to bring you back to this place. For I know the plans I have for you," declares the Lord, "plans to prosper you and not to harm you, *plans to give you hope and a future.* (emphasis added) Then you will call on me and come and pray to me, and I will listen to you. You will seek me and find me when you seek me with all your heart. I will be found by you," declares the Lord, "and will bring you back from captivity."
(*NIV*, Jeremiah 29:4-7, 10-14)

- The Prophet Jeremiah

The community I see is a place where:
- *Crime rates begin to drop*
- *Meth loses its power*
- *Sex trafficking ends*
- *Churches work together on common issues*
- *Nonprofits have the resources they need to make a difference*
- *Racism is no more*
- *Leaders from various sectors work together to address issues*
- *Employment increases*
- *Need for public assistance decreases*
- *Networks of people across socioeconomic lines work together*
- *Innovative businesses thrive*
- *Artists create meaningful works of art*
- *Amazing coffee shops and vegan restaurants are on every corner (Hey, this is my dream. I might as well be honest.)*
- *Churches grow with increasingly healthy people*
- *Poverty loses its control*
- *Those who were once in poverty lead community organizations*
- *Every single neighborhood is safe to walk through at night*
- *Every person understands God's love for them*
- *Every person understands the value and worth they have*
- *Life and love are flourishing*

A community of hope.

Fight poverty
and strengthen
families with us.
A great way to
start is to
take a tour.

Schedule your tour today at

restoringpeople.com/tour

About the
Evansville Christian Life Center

The Evansville Christian Life Center is a nonprofit organization in
Evansville, Indiana, working to restore people from need to potential in Christ.

We dream of a community with less poverty and stronger families,
and work toward making that happen.

We provide a three-step path to restoration:
- *Relief (meeting practical needs like food and clothing)*
- *Resource (offering education and relationships)*
- *Release (in-depth and long-term anti-poverty initiative)*

You can join the work as a volunteer and a donor.
A great first step is to take a 60-minute tour.
Follow us on Facebook, Instagram, Snapchat, and Twitter: @restoringpeople

Learn more at restoringpeople.com.

About the authors

GINA GIBSON

Gina has served as the Executive Director/CEO of the Evansville Christian Life Center since 2006. When she's not working, playing golf, or making kale smoothies, you'll usually find her spending time with her grandkids. She and her husband, Greg, have two sons, two daughters-in-law and four granddaughters.

JEREMY SECREST

Jeremy serves as the Director of Marketing at the Evansville Christian Life Center. He has written several books, including the ECLC's *Jeremiah Jettison* kids' series. In his spare time, you'll find him reading, writing, or taking walks with his family. He and his wife, Joy, have three kids.

38162807R00035

Made in the USA
Middletown, DE
09 March 2019